Building Character

Being Honest

by Rebecca Pettiford

Bullfrog Books

Ideas for Parents and Teachers

Bullfrog Books let children practice reading informational text at the earliest reading levels. Repetition, familiar words, and photo labels support early readers.

Before Reading

- Discuss the cover photo. What does it tell them?
- Look at the picture glossary together. Read and discuss the words.

Read the Book

- "Walk" through the book and look at the photos. Let the child ask questions. Point out the photo labels.
- Read the book to the child, or have him or her read independently.

After Reading

- Prompt the child to think more. Ask: How important is honesty to you? Is it hard to be honest? Or does it come naturally?

Bullfrog Books are published by Jump!
5357 Penn Avenue South
Minneapolis, MN 55419
www.jumplibrary.com

Library of Congress Cataloging-in-Publication Data

Names: Pettiford, Rebecca, author.
Title: Being honest / by Rebecca Pettiford.
Description: Minneapolis, MN: Jump!, Inc., [2017]
Series: Building character | Audience: K to Grade 3.
Audience: Age: 5–8. | Includes index.
Identifiers: LCCN 2017023777 (print)
LCCN 2017023019 (ebook)
ISBN 9781624966439 (ebook)
ISBN 9781620318782 (hardcover: alk. paper)
ISBN 9781620318799 (pbk.)
Subjects: LCSH: Honesty—Juvenile literature.
Classification: LCC BF723.H7 (print) | LCC BF723.
H7 P48 2017 (ebook) | DDC 179/.9—dc23
LC record available at https://lccn.loc.gov/2017023777

Editor: Kirsten Chang
Book Designer: Michelle Sonnek
Photo Researcher: Michelle Sonnek

Photo Credits: Koraysa/iStock, cover; michaeljung/Shutterstock, 1; Bo Valentino/Shutterstock, 3; wavebreakmedia/Shutterstock, 4; Chad Zuber/Shutterstock, 5; Pierre Yu/Shutterstock, 6–7; Zurijeta/Shutterstock, 8–9; Gelpi/Shutterstock, 10 (foreground); science photo/Shutterstock, 10 (background); MyImages - Micha/Shutterstock, 11, 23bl; Wavebreakmedia/iStock, 12–13; photastic/Shutterstock, 14; Monkey Business Images/Shutterstock, 14–15; Blend Images/Shutterstock, 16–17; Kues/Shutterstock, 18 (foreground); romakoma/Shutterstock, 18 (background); Kulniz/Shutterstock, 19, 23br; Dragon Images/Shutterstock, 20–21; Michael Smolkin/Shutterstock, 22; Roman Pelesh/Shutterstock, 23tl; Zadorozhnyi Viktor/Shutterstock, 23tr; i7do/Shutterstock, 24; Samuel Borges Photography/Shutterstock, 24 (boy).

Printed in the United States of America at Corporate Graphics in North Mankato, Minnesota.

Table of Contents

Tell the Truth

We should
be honest.

This means to
tell the truth.

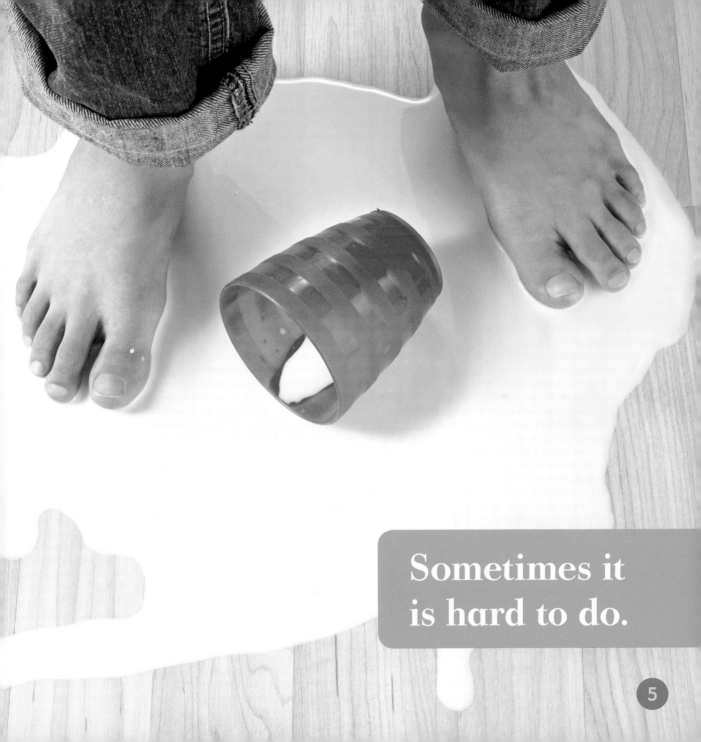

Sometimes it
is hard to do.

vase

Crash! Dell breaks a vase.

He tells his mom.
She is not mad. Why?
Dell told the truth.

Oh, no! Zoe lost
a library book.

She tells her dad.
They pay the fine.

Max likes Joe's kite.

But he does not take it.

He asks to borrow it.

Joe says yes!

We play games.

Leo keeps score.

He could give himself more points.

But does he? No.

He is honest.

Leo |||
Mom ||
Ali ||||

Time for a quiz!

Nick does not cheat.

He is proud of his grade.

Lucy finds
Mr. Lee's wallet.

She gives it to him.

He thanks her.

It feels good
to be honest!

Picture the Truth

Honesty is about being truthful. This book showed different ways to be truthful. Asking to borrow a toy and telling the truth about breaking something are two examples from the book. Do you have a favorite example? You could also think of one that is not in the book. Draw a picture of it, and put yourself in the picture. Hang it in your room so you can see it every day. It will help you remember how important it is to be honest.

You will need:
- a clean sheet of paper
- colored markers or crayons
- stickers (optional)

Picture Glossary

cheat
To behave in a dishonest way to gain something you want.

vase
A container used for flowers or as decoration.

fine
Money that you have to pay as a punishment.

wallet
A small folding case that holds paper money and bank cards.

Index

To Learn More

Learning more is as easy as 1, 2, 3.

1) Go to www.factsurfer.com

2) Enter "beinghonest" into the search box.

3) Click the "Surf" button to see a list of websites.

With factsurfer.com, finding more information is just a click away.